Explore the Legend of King Arthur

Written and Illustrated by

Alix Wood

King Arthur and the Knights of the Round Table have been written about by many people over many centuries. This book retells the stories and investigates the sites and the facts and the fiction. Dice, a pen and a small mirror will be useful to complete some of the puzzles and games. There are many tales and places connected with King Arthur. The author has chosen some of her favourites.

The Sword in the Stone

When Arthur was born he was in danger. Arthur's half-sisters, the witch Morgana le Fay and her two evil sisters, wanted to kill him. His parents, Uther and Igraine Pendragon needed to protect the future King. They pretended Arthur had died and Merlin the wizard took little Arthur to live with Sir Ector and his son, Kay. Merlin came to see Arthur fifteen years after his father Uther had died. The country had suffered many wars as there was no king to take Uther's place and rule. "The time has come", said Merlin.

At the Grand Tournament in London there was a Great Council meeting to decide a new King. There was a stone that held an anvil with a beautiful sword stuck in it. On the stone it said "Who pulleth out this sword from this stone and anvil is rightwise born King of England". No one could pull it out. Kay had left his sword behind and was about to fight in the Tournament. Arthur went to get it for him, but got lost in the crowds. He stumbled upon the stone, and pulled out the magical sword with ease.

Dot-to-dot

Join the dots starting at number 1 and find out what is stuck in the anvil

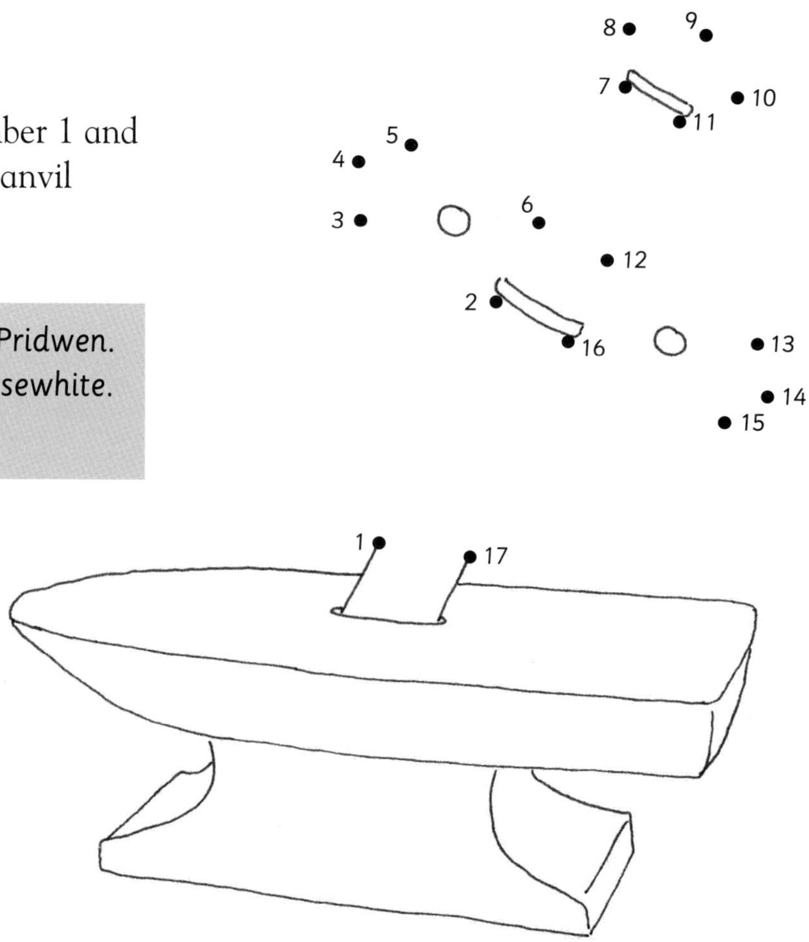

Arthur had a shield called Pridwen.
His helmet was named Goosewhite.
His lance was called Ron!

Tintagel - Arthur's Birthplace?

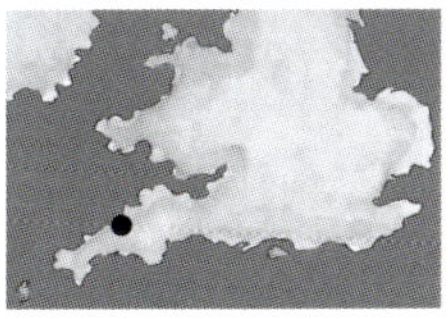

Tintagel in North Cornwall is a beautiful strange place. The ruined castle on the cliffs was built around 1230. People thought it was the site of an older monastery too. But Mediterranean pottery recently found shows it was really an important, possibly royal, site of a Cornish chieftain! But was it Arthur's birthplace?

In 1998, a broken piece of Cornish slate with the name "Artognov" was found by archaeologist Kevin Brady. He said "As the stone came out, when I saw the letters A-R-T, I thought uh-oh..." The stone has been dated to the time when Arthur was said to live. Is Artognov Arthur? Artognov would have been pronounced Arthnou in 600. The stone at least shows that the name Arthur was used at that time.

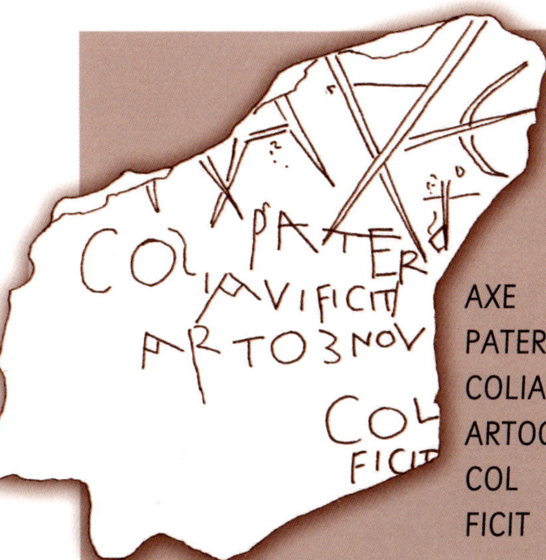

AXE
PATER
COLIAVIFICIT
ARTOGNOU
COL
FICIT

The "Arthur" stone inscriptions read: AXE = possibly Emperor Maxentius? PATER COLIAVIFICIT ARTOGNOU COL FICIT = "Artognou father of a descendant of Coll has had this made". We can only guess what the rest of the stone said.

Spot the differences

Can you find the 11 differences in the two drawings of Tintagel?

Can you find Merlin's Cave? It is filled by the sea twice a day, and is said to be haunted by Merlin's ghost. At low tide you can walk through the cave. Look closely and you'll find a seam where smugglers used to hide.

Camelot

Few believed a boy could be a good King. Some followed Arthur, but others were jealous and prepared to fight him. One of the first things Arthur did was to knight Sir Kay and make Ector his protector, to thank them for looking after him when he was younger.

Arthur built his castle at Camelot and tried to bring peace to the country, but peace was hard to find. Arthur's enemy, King Pellinore, was attacking King Leodegraunce in Wales. Arthur knew he must kill rebel King Pellinore. During the fierce fight, Morgana Le Fay made Arthur weak with a spell and his sword shattered, but Merlin helped Arthur kill the rebel king.

Leodegraunce's daughter Guinevere was beautiful and Arthur fell in love with her. Merlin warned him not to marry her. Merlin said mysteriously "You threaten Camelot and your own life with Guinevere as queen".

Rocky Valley Maze

This strange maze is carved on a wall in the Rocky Valley, Tintagel, Cornwall. There are two of these petroglyphs (rock carvings) there. They are thousands of years old. Exactly the same labyrinth is found carved all over the world. Some think it is a map of the legendary sunken city of Atlantis, because it looks like a description of it in a very old book. Arthur may have seen this maze on his travels.

Help Arthur find the treasure by following the maze.

More about sunken cities later in this book!

Camelot ~ Where was it?

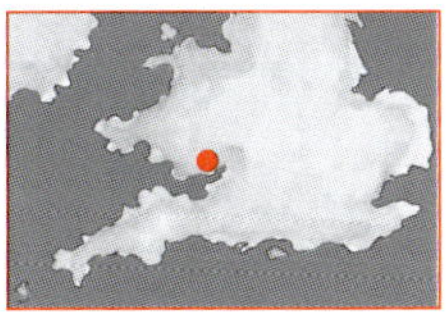

Wales? Geoffrey of Monmouth lived near Caerleon, a large Roman town. His book 'History of the Kings of Britain' says Arthur held court at Caerleon. Nearby 'Caerwent' translates into English as 'Winchester' where Malory thought Camelot was. Caerwent was an important place around the time of King Arthur. It's said a monastery was established there with permission from Caradoc, one of King Arthur's knights.

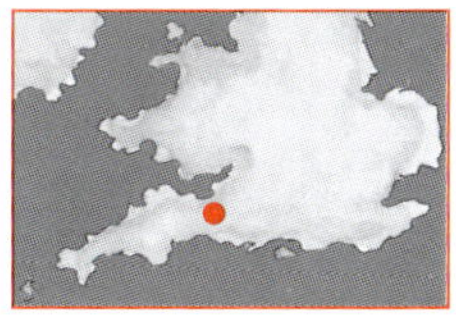

Somerset? In 1542 scholar John Leland said South Cadbury was Camelot. It is very old and at the time of Arthur it was a town with 4 massive walls, made from stone from old Roman buildings. Legend says that the hill is hollow and Arthur and his knights are asleep inside. The hill is limestone, so may well have a cave. One night a year, a ghostly Arthur and his men are said to ride down to a stream to let their horses drink. The Somerset village of Queen Camel near South Cadbury is also thought by some to be Camelot.

Shadow match

Arthur is walking home in the dark. Which shadow is the same shape as Arthur's hut at Camelot?

a

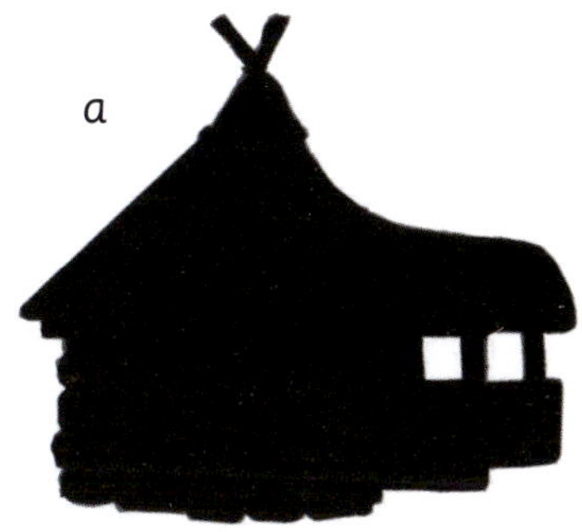

b c

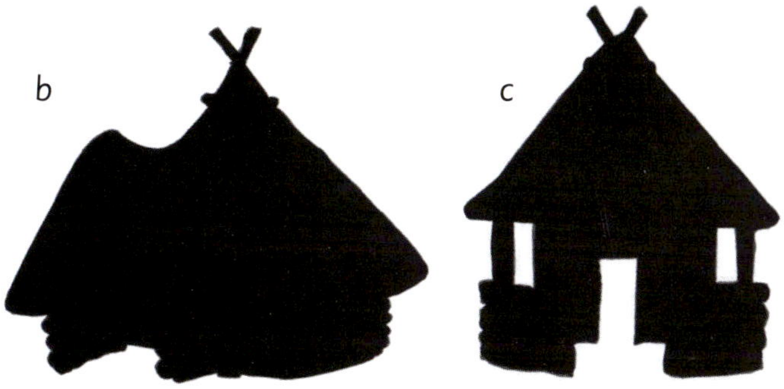

d e

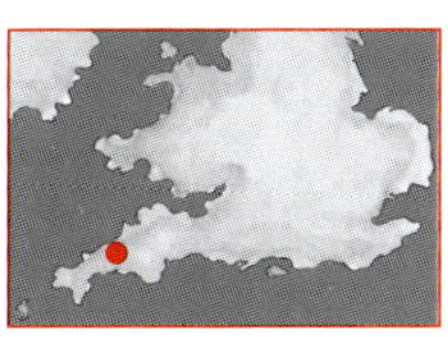

Cornwall? If Camelot is in Cornwall most people think it is at Kelly Rounds (also called Castle Killibury) near Wadebridge. Welsh sources call Camelot "Celliwig". Some pot fragments have been found at Kelly Rounds which means it was used in Arthur's time. Another possible site is Castle Canyke, a huge hill fort at Bodmin, 2km south of a property called 'Callywith'. Could that be Celliwig? The town of Callington, in Cornish 'Kelliwik', also has a claim.

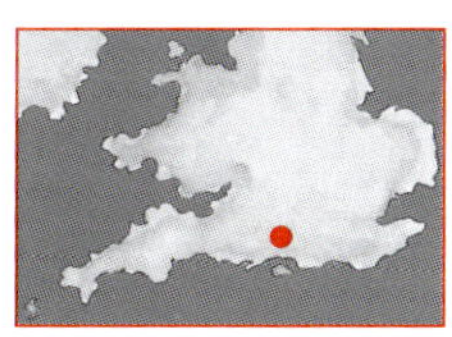

Hampshire? Winchester is the choice of Sir Thomas Malory. In his 'Le Morte D'Arthur' (1469) he placed Camelot there, "..and within five days' journey they came to Camelot, that is called in English, Winchester". But could it really be Caerwent?

Excalibur

Arthur was worried his magic sword was broken. Merlin said it had served its purpose, and took Arthur through a thick forest to the mysterious Lake of Avalon, to look for the magic sword Excalibur. Arthur shouted "I am Arthur, King of England. I seek the sword Excalibur," and out of the lake appeared a hand holding a sword. Up rose the figure of Nimue, the Lady of the Lake. She told Arthur to use the sword wisely and never to be parted from it. Merlin then gave him a scabbard to put the sword in. "This will keep you from harm." Arthur buckled it to his waist.

Arthur examined the beautiful sword. On one side was written " Keep me!" and on the other "Throw me away!" Merlin explained that the sword was his only for his lifetime — when death came, he must throw the sword back into the lake.

Back in the woods Merlin disappeared. Arthur rested, drowsy by the fire, looking forward to seeing Guinevere — and suddenly he felt she was bending to kiss him, as if in a dream. Falling asleep, he felt Excalibur hum and realised it wasn't Guinevere. He swung his sword around him. Evil Morgana le Fay and the witches stole his scabbard as Arthur swung Excalibur wildly. Morgana cried "Without this you will bleed as any mortal. I shall stand over you one day as you bleed your life blood. Then your kingdom will be my kingdom!"

Merlin Scrabble

How many new words can you make from the name Merlin? Use each letter only once in each word. It is written in a circle to help you.

E

M R

N

I L

Excalibur and the Lady of the Lake

Excalibur, first called Caliburn, is said to have been forged in Avalon out of stone.

Offerings were often thrown into lakes to please the gods. We still throw money into wishing wells for the same reason.

Dozmary Pool, or Loe Pool, both in Cornwall, are believed to be Excalibur's lake. In Somerset, there is Pomparles Bridge (or Pont Perilous Bridge). It is between Glastonbury and Street, but the old bridge has been replaced with a new one.

Colour me in

Arthur and The Round Table

Arthur decided to marry his beloved Guinevere despite Merlin's warning. Her father, Leodegraunce, gave them a beautiful round table, with 150 richly carved chairs as a wedding present. The magician Merlin had made the table long ago for Arthur's father. Merlin found 28 knights worthy to sit at the Round Table and Leodegraunce gave him 100 of his finest knights too. Together they would build a new kingdom, The Kingdom of Logres. Each knight swore an oath "I will protect the weak, show mercy to those who ask, and perform only deeds that show honour to the table, the kingdom and God".

As each knight took his seat, magically his name appeared in gold on the back of his chair. Eventually all but one chair had a knight's name written in gold. On that last chair was written the word "Perilous". The knights all wondered who that chair was for.

Merlin told Arthur he must leave, rest and save his strength. Merlin foretold "I will wake again, but far in the future, when Logres most needs me. Fear those close to you. Morgana le Fay will try and destroy you. Your greatest test will be on the field called Camlann."

Knight's Code of Chivalry

A Knight must obey the sacred oaths of chivalry. The code had strict rules of etiquette (manners) and conduct. Can you match the oath to its definition, and become a Knight of the Round Table?

Oath	Definition
PROWESS	Faithfulness
JUSTICE	Skill in battle
LOYALTY	Generosity
LARGESSE	Being fair and reasonable
COURAGE	Noble birth or fine qualities
NOBILITY	Bravery
HUMILITY	Protecting from attack
DEFENCE	Modesty

King Arthur - Fact or Fiction?

The Winchester Round Table

This round table is hanging in the Great Hall at Winchester Castle. Is it King Arthur's?

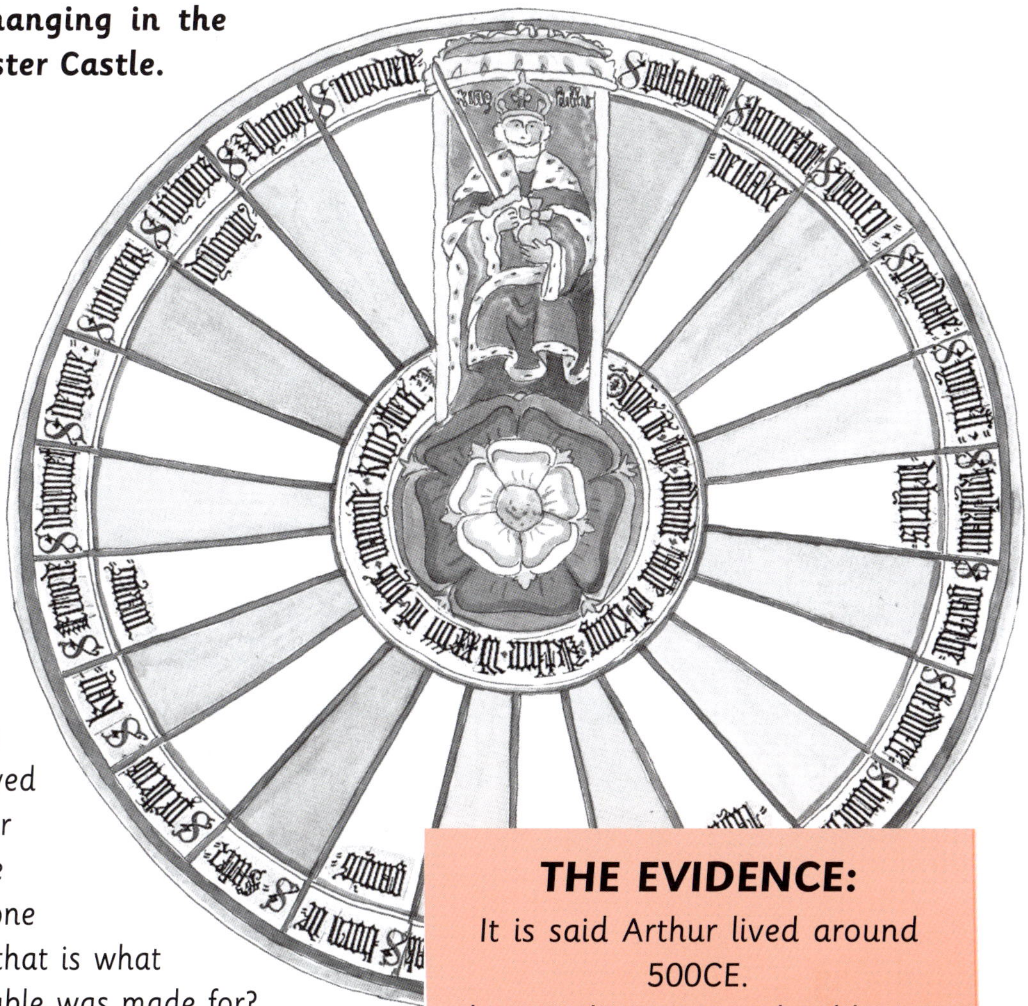

This table is very old; experts who can tell the age of wooden objects say it was made between 1250–1280, when Edward I was King. Festivals called Round Tables were held in Europe then. There was jousting, dancing and feasting. Sometimes the knights pretended to be Arthur's knights. King Edward loved the stories of King Arthur and went to at least five Round Tables and held one himself in 1299. Maybe that is what the Winchester Round Table was made for?

The painting on the table is much newer; it was done for King Henry VIII of England when the Holy Roman Emperor Charles V visited in 1522, and shows Henry himself sitting in Arthur's seat above a Tudor rose.

THE EVIDENCE:

It is said Arthur lived around 500CE.

The Winchester Round Table was made around 1270CE

Can it be Arthur's?

yes or no

Magic Writing

Work some Merlin magic and find out which knight should sit at each chair?

Lancelot Arrives

A baby was abandoned at the castle that night. Arthur and Guinevere fostered him and called him Mordred. Another baby was in need that night too. Merlin knew that King Ban of Benwick would die in battle the next day. He asked the Lady of the Lake to foster his son. His name was Lancelot and he and his son after him would be the best of all knights. Merlin left with Nimue, the Lady of the Lake. A magical underground passage opened up for them. Merlin lay on a large flat stone inside and went to sleep. Nimue closed the passage behind her as she left.

Some time later, a knight arrived on a stretcher at the Court of Camelot, a sword blade broken off deep in his thigh. He had been told by a hermit that a knight at Camelot could pull the blade from his leg. He would be the most noble and best of all knights. One by one, the knights tried and failed. At that moment Nimue arrived with Lancelot and she explained who he was. Arthur at once knighted him. Sir Lancelot then pulled the blade from the wounded knight's leg and the knight was healed. Guinevere was entranced by Lancelot. Nimue noticed, and smiled sadly. This was the beginning of the end.

Lancelot went to sit at the table. Would he sit at the seat marked "Perilous"? No, he stopped one seat short.

Merlin the Shape-Shifter

Merlin often disguised himself to confuse people. Follow the trail to see which of these animals Merlin has disguised himself as.

MERLIN

Merlin is said to be the son of a demon and a nun, and gets his great powers from the forces of good and evil. There are many stories about him.

Merlin first proved himself as a boy. Geoffrey of Monmouth says King Vortigern was building a fort on a mountain in North Wales against the invading Anglo-Saxons. Each time the fort was nearly finished, it mysteriously collapsed. Vortigern's advisors suggested a boy must be sacrificed to stop the curse, and they picked young Merlin. Just as Merlin was about to die, he told the king that the problem was two dragons in a pool, in the cave below the fort. The pool was discovered and the dragons released. Vortigern was so impressed by Merlin's mystic knowledge that he made him his chief advisor.

Dragon Match

Draw lines to join the matching dragons. Which is the odd one out?

a

b

c

d

e

Lancelot and Elaine

Lancelot was so good and brave in battle, other knights lost courage when they fought him. Guinevere said he should fight the next tournament in disguise, so he did not put off the other knights. Lancelot agreed, and set off for the next tournament in disguise. On the way he asked for shelter at Astolat. He entertained King Pelles with stories of his brave adventures and the king's daughter Elaine listened in awe. Elaine fell in love with the mysterious knight. To improve his disguise, he swapped his shield, and Elaine persuaded him to wear her favour. Lancelot reluctantly agreed. He loved Guinevere and usually wore her favour.

Lancelot fought bravely and won the contest, but was injured. He headed home before claiming his prize. Gawain searched for the mysterious winner. He asked at Astolat, and Elaine showed Gawain her mysterious visitor's shield. He recognised it at once. They found injured Lancelot, and Elaine nursed Lancelot back to health. When he was better, Lancelot was grateful, but longed to return to Camelot. He left without saying goodbye.

Elaine was heartbroken. Unknown to Lancelot she was expecting his child. Feeling weak, she asked the nuns to look after her baby, and told her father "When I am dead, lay me in a boat and send it floating down to Camelot. Put this note in my hand". Then she died and her father's grief turned Astolat into a windy wasteland. Arthur read the note, "You left me without farewell, Lancelot du Lac, so I have come to make my last goodbye to you. I, Elaine, maid of Astolat who loved you, and who had no love in return."

The Lady of Shalott

In Tennyson's poem "The Lady of Shalott" Elaine is cursed to never look out of her window, she can only see the world with a mirror. One day, Lancelot passes. She forgets the curse and looks at him. Her mirror cracks, and she is cursed. She goes to the river, lies in a boat and dies as she floats to Camelot.

Magic Mirrors

Put a small mirror between the dotted lines on the left and slowly drag it along the picture to the right. Circle anyone you see hiding!

Lancelot at the Tournament

Torre, Elaine's brother, lent Lancelot his plain white shield. Can you find him at the Tournament?

Mordred and Galahad

People noticed Mordred looked like Arthur, with his pale blue eyes and brown hair. Arthur had made Mordred a knight, but Mordred felt most at home in the dark forest. It was there that he once met a woman sitting by a bubbling pot. She greeted Mordred and said "I have watched you since you arrived at Camelot, I knew your mother, and I knew your father too". Mordred thought he knew this strange woman. She began to tell him about his life. "Arthur is my father? So I am his heir?" Morgana le Fay told him to be silent for now, and the time would come.

A man ran into the Great Hall during dinner and shouted that he had seen a stone floating in the river with a sword in it. The knights rushed to the river and saw a red marble stone. In it was a sword, engraved with "No man shall draw me but the purest knight of all." Lancelot was called, but he blushed thinking of Guinevere and Elaine and said "No". They searched the castle and found the nuns in the Great Hall with a young man who was tall and proud and his armour shone like a suit of light. He had no sword, just a scarlet shield. "He is Galahad, son of Lancelot and Elaine", the nuns told Arthur. Everyone gasped. Lancelot came up to see him more clearly. Galahad walked around the table and stopped by the last empty seat, once marked "Perilous". Lifting the silk covering, there was his name, in gold!

They went to the river and Arthur ordered Galahad to take the sword, which he did with ease, and Arthur knighted him by the riverside.

Cross out

Cross out the letters that appear more than once in the grid. Write the letters left over in the shields. Galahad's treasure is jumbled up in the letters

O	T	F	H	S
G	W	D	V	E
A	H	L	R	O
F	P	W	I	S
T	D	V	E	P

Write your answer here

arthur in: Somerset

In King Arthur's time Somerset was known as the summer region because the moors and levels were great summer grazing, but under water in winter.

Brent Knoll - In 'The Antiquities of Glastonbury' by William of Malmesbury, Arthur sent Yder to fight three giants at Brentecnol. He slayed the giants and fell concussed. Arthur arrived and thought Yder was dead. Feeling guilty he made 80 monks pray for Yder's soul and gave lands including Brent Knoll to the abbey. An island-like hill, Brent Knoll has an old earthwork at the top. It was in use in Roman times and there was a small fort in the 13th century. It may form part of a beacon chain between South Cadbury, Glastonbury Tor and Dinas Powys in Wales.

Bath - Arthur fought 12 battles between 485-496. The Battle of Badon Hill was his greatest triumph. This almost total defeat of the Saxons brought a time of peace to Britain. Many locate the Battle of Badon Hill near the city of Bath, either at Little Solsbury Hill or

Mount Badon. Nennius, writing in the 800s, seems to say that Bath and Badon are the same place.

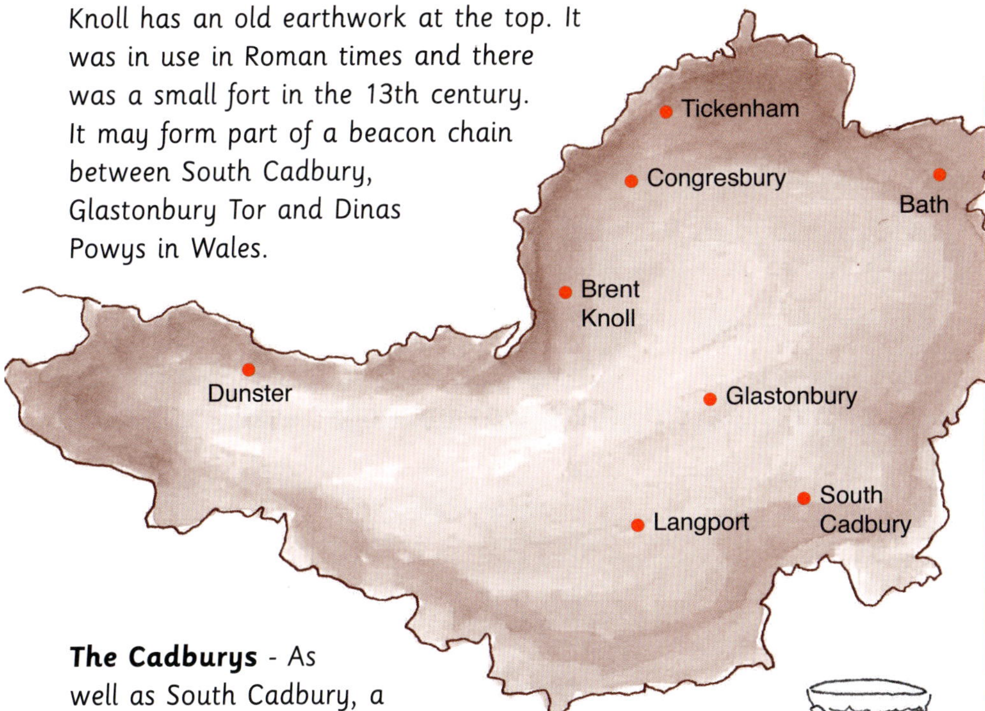

THE EVIDENCE:

- More than one book says Arthur was in Somerset
- His body was supposed to be discovered at Glastonbury
- He maybe fought a big battle at Bath

Was Arthur in Somerset, what do you think?

yes or no

The Cadburys - As well as South Cadbury, a potential site for Camelot, there is Cadbury Camp at Tickenham in Somerset and Cadbury Hill at Congresbury. Cadbury Hill was occupied in Arthur's time and probably Cadbury Camp was too, but that doesn't prove an Arthur connection. It's possible the name Cadbury comes from Cadwy's bury, in which case all three might be associated with Arthur as some books say Arthur and Cadwy shared the reign of Dumnonia at Dunster. Some think Cadwy is another name for Ector's son Kay, who protected Arthur when he was a boy.

Glastonbury - It is believed Joseph of Arimathea brought the holy grail back to Glastonbury. It has been a holy site for many centuries. Glastonbury is also believed by many to be Avalon, the magical place where Arthur is sleeping. Monks claimed to have found the tomb of Arthur in 1190 and Guinevere is believed to have been imprisoned on the Tor. More about that on page 31.

Langport - There is an old Welsh poem in the 'Black Book of Carmarthen' about Geraint which mentions the king of Dumnonia fighting with 'Arthur's brave men' at Llongborth (probably Langport by the River Parrett). In winter the surrounding marshes were flooded. Langport was the easiest crossing point.

Arthur's Quest

Land on as many treasures as you can on your journey to Avalon. Play by yourself or challenge your friends. Whoever finishes with the most treasure wins. If it is a tie, who finishes first wins.

You need counters, and a die or spinner to play, and a pen and paper to note the treasures won, like this.

	Me	Them
Excalibur		
Crown		
Ring		
Lance		
Jewel		
Cloak		
Helmet		
Shield		
Grail		

start

Tintagel

TREASURE **Excalibur**

Merlin enchants you Go forward 3

Hurt in tournament Go back 3

Drink potion Float forward 3

Camelot

Morgana tricks you Go back 3

TREASURE **Crown**

the woods

monastery

Excalibur glows Go forward 3

Lost your sword Go back 3

TREASURE **Ring**

Merlin's cave

Win a joust Go forward 3

Rocky Valley

Stuck in the Maze Go back 3

the tournament

Brent Knoll

Merlin helps you Go back and get one missed treasure or stay on this square

TREASURE **Lance**

Dragon ahead Go back 3

Caerleon
Treasure
Jewel
Merlin helps you
Go forward 3
Fighting a serpent
Go back 3
Winchester
the Wasteland
Treasure
Cloak
Mordred appears
Go back 3
Follow Nimue
Go forward 3
St Leven
Treasure
Helmet
Glastonbury
Long church service
Go back 3
Bodmin Moor
Jump on a horse
Go forward 3
Lost in the mist
Go back 3
Astolat
Hermitage
Hermit heals you
Go forward 3
Lyonesse
Treasure
Shield
Slaughter Bridge
Merlin helps fight
Go forward 3
Dozmary Pool
Injured at Camlann
Go back 3
Treasure
Grail
Merlin helps you
Go back and get one missed treasure or stay on this square
Avalon

The Quest for the Holy Grail

Lancelot was delighted to find his son but he was filled with worry. Suddenly the wind picked up to a gale and Camelot was lit up with a strange light. Over the round table an object, covered by a cloth, hovered, then vanished. "The Holy Grail", said Galahad. "The cup which Jesus drank from at the Last Supper. We are not fit to see its beauty. The vision is asking us to find it".

Galahad and Lancelot went looking for the Grail. Lancelot hoped he would get to know his new-found son and find forgiveness for his love of Guinevere. Gawain and many other knights volunteered too, and at first light, they left the castle, splitting into groups of two or three. Guinevere cried as she watched the knights disappear into the distance.

One by one the knights returned until only four remained, Lancelot, Bors, Percival and Galahad. They had been on their quest for many months, been separated and gone through many hardships. Lancelot found himself in the Wastelands, and sought shelter in the doorway of the chapel. He did not realise in his sleepiness that it was Astolat. The other three knights arrived too at the Castle. King Pelles was happy to see them, but still sad at the death of his daughter, Elaine. His land was a windy desert still, and he was in pain from a cut leg that wouldn't heal.

Merlin's Rock

Merlin predicted the Spanish invasion of Cornwall! In the bay at Mousehole in Cornwall lies Merlin's Rock. An old Cornish poem about the rock says:

**"There shall land on the rock of Merlin
Those who shall burn Paul, Penzance and Newlyn"**

Astonishingly, this is exactly what happened in 1595 when the Spanish invaded and burnt all but the manor house to the ground! Outside the house is a plaque saying "Squire Jenkyn Keigwin was killed here 23rd July 1595 defending this house against the Spaniards".

Can you read Cornish?

Here is the poem in Cornish. Can you tell which word means 'and'?

Ewra teyre a war meane Merlyn
Ara lesky Pawle Pensanz ha Newlyn

arthur in: Cornwall

Bossiney - near Tintagel, there is a mound, probably the remains of castle motte, or burial mound. Tradition says the Round Table is buried there, and on midsummer night it rises, a flash of light lights up the sky, and the gold table sinks again.

Bodmin Moor - Site of King Arthur's Bed, a rocky outcrop and King Arthur's Downs. King Arthur's Hall is on the Downs near St Breward, an ancient perhaps prehistoric structure. It is a rectangular bank with stones placed vertically around the inner edge, once thought to be the chair backs of Arthur's knights.

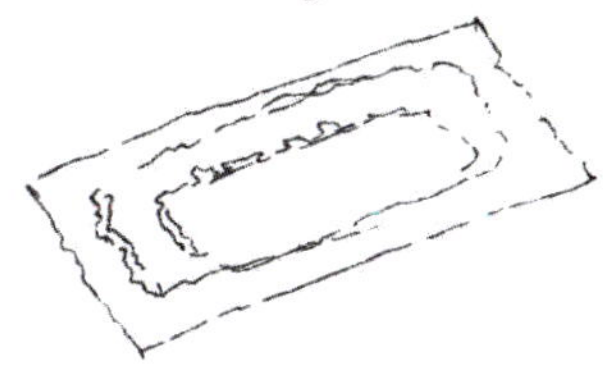

Camelford - Slaughterbridge is believed to be the battlefield Camlann. A stone found there is inscribed "Latini hic iacit filius Ma[   ]ri" Some think the gap said 'Magni Arturi' so the stone says 'Here lies Latinus, son of Arthur the Great'.

Trevethy Quoit, or King Arthur's Quoit, is an impressive Bronze Age burial chamber. The top stone is mysteriously pierced by a hole. The front entrance stone was cut, perhaps to leave an entrance into the chamber?

St Levan - In the churchyard is St Levan's stone. It must have been precious when the church was built, or it would have been used in the building. Arthur is said to have come here with Merlin long before St Levan's time and Merlin prophesied—

"When, with panniers astride,
A pack-horse one can ride
Through St Levan stone,
The world will be done."

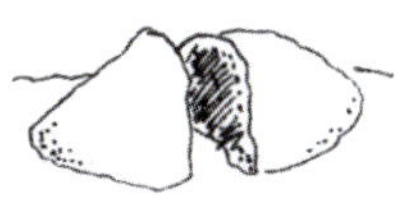

Others say it was St Levan who said it.

St Endellion's patron saint, Endelienta, lived on cows' milk. One day her cow went onto the lord of Trenteny's field and the neighbour killed the cow. King Arthur was Endelienta's godfather, and angry, he killed the neighbour. Endelienta thought that a bit harsh, and revived him.

Can you read Ogham?

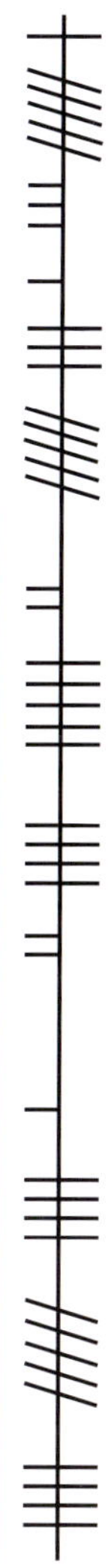

Can you write Ogham?

The Arthur Stone at Slaughterbridge also carries a 'hidden' inscription, not in Latin but in an Irish script called Ogham. It's believed to be a secret language created to send messages among the druids. It is this script which dates the stone to the 6th Century, the time of Arthur. Ogham characters are cut into one edge of the Stone. Unfortunately the text is very worn but appears to repeat the name LATINI.

There are 20 letters in the Ogham alphabet, so some are missing. Draw a vertical line on paper, and then put the marks down the line to write your coded message!

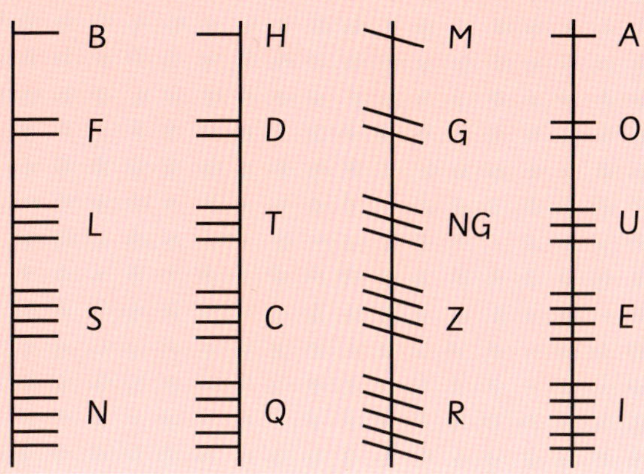

Maidens of the Grail

Suddenly, the howling wind stopped, and the huge doors to the castle opened slowly. Three young women dressed in white walked silently towards them. The first carried a candlestick. The second had a spear, dripping drops of blood, which vanished as they hit the ground. The third carried a golden dish. Behind them, blinding like sunlight floated a fourth woman, carrying a small table with an object covered in a silk cloth. "It must be the Grail, our quest is nearly over", thought Galahad.

Lancelot woke up in the doorway of the chapel, and found he could not move. He could not speak. The procession passed by and into the chapel and the door slammed shut behind them. Lancelot was left alone outside.

Inside, Galahad took the spear and said "This spear pierced Christ's side when he was on the cross. The blood is his blood." He let a few drops fall onto Pelles leg and his cut healed instantly. At the same moment, the crumbling castle was rebuilt and the wasteland became full of flowers again. The woman took the cover off the Grail and Galahad knelt and put the grail to his lips. A shaft of light struck Galahad and he seemed to disappear. Outside, Lancelot saw a bright light, and then was plunged into darkness.

Missing jigsaw piece

Find the piece which completes Mordred's shield.

a

b

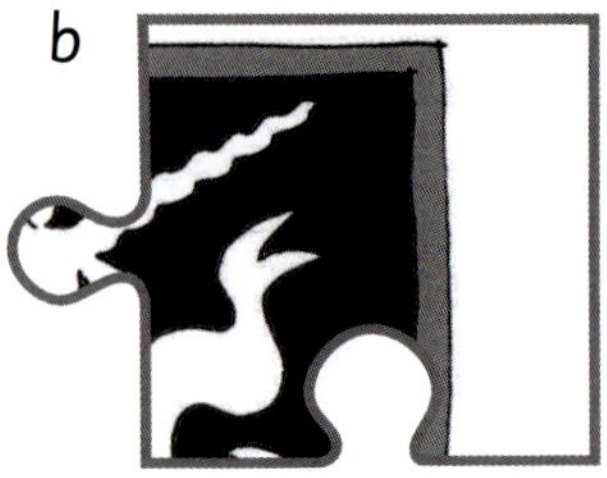

c

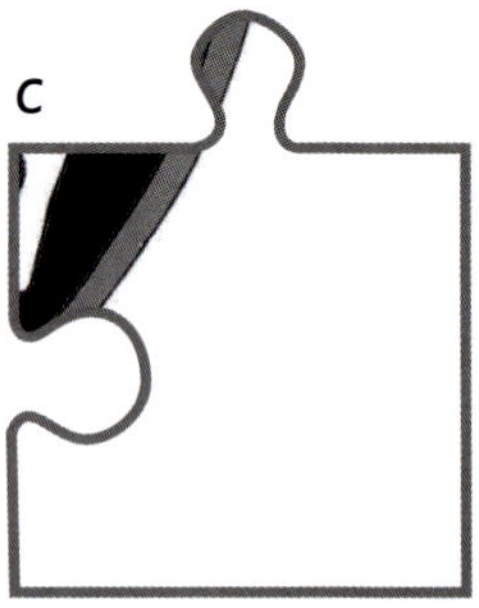

d

e

tristan and iseult

Sir Tristan of Lyonesse was one of the Knights of King Arthur's Round Table.

His name means sorrow, as his mother died giving birth to him. He lived with his Uncle, King Mark. To thank King Mark and Tristan for help in battle, King Anguish gave his daughter Iseult in marriage to King Mark. Tristan was sent to Ireland to bring her to Cornwall.

Iseult's mother gave her a love potion for her wedding night. Iseult and Tristan accidentally drank it, and fell in love. Iseult still married Mark but loved Tristan. Mark found out about their love and banned Tristan from his castle. Tristan went to King Arthur's Court and then France, and married Iseult of Brittany, because her name reminded him of his love. When Tristan became ill, he sent a message to Cornwall asking Iseult to come to him. To signal to him if she was on the returning ship, the sails should be white, and if she was not coming, they should be black. On his sick bed he asked Iseult of Brittany what colour the sails were as the ship approached. She lied and said black. He died of sadness, then when Iseult arrived, she too died of grief.

Castle Dore

Near Fowey in Cornwall, Castle Dore is believed to be King Mark's castle. Béroul, a 12th century poet, says Mark lived at Lancien. There is a Lantyan Farm, 2km north of the castle, spelt Lantien in 1086. In the poem Iseult walks on a paved road from there to a monastery at St Samson. There is a church at Golant called St Sampson, 2km east of the Castle! 6th Century post holes have been found at the castle, and much earlier artefacts too.

THE EVIDENCE:

—◇— The Saints' Way from Padstow to Fowey was used in Arthur's time by traders, drovers and pilgrims travelling from Ireland and Wales to Europe avoiding the dangerous sea around Land's End.

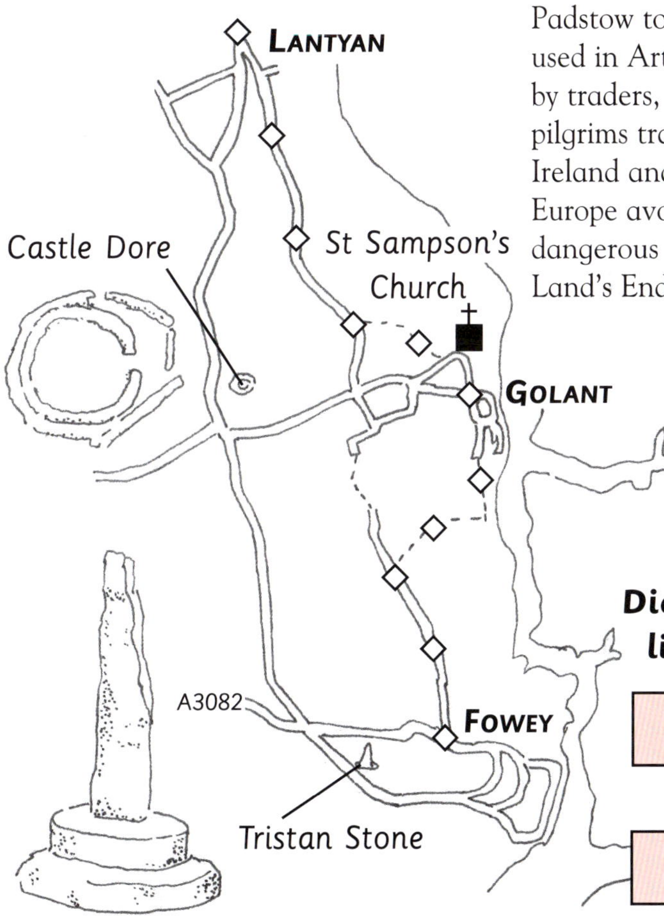

Did Tristan live here?

yes

or

no

Is this Tristan's gravestone?

An ancient stone, 7ft (2.13m) high, set in a newer millstone base, was found near the castle. Carved into it, it says in Latin: **'Drustanus lies here, the son of Cunomorus'.** People think 'Drustanus' is Tristan and 'Cunomorus' is Marcus Cunomorus (King Mark). There is a strong possiblity that King Mark and Tristan existed, with the king having castles at Tintagel and Castle Dore. Originally the stone was much closer to Castle Dore but it was moved.

Mordred Traps Lancelot

When the knights returned to Camelot, they told everyone of their adventure. Except Lancelot, he said sadly that he had been too sinful to see. He felt everyone stare at him, and Mordred smiled. He knew why Lancelot felt guilty. He had followed Lancelot and Guinevere often with his brother Sir Agravain, trying to catch them together.

One day he asked Morgana le Fay for help. Arthur overheard Mordred and Agravain discussing the matter and would not believe that Lancelot and Guinevere had betrayed him. Mordred said he could show him proof. They heard laughter that sounded like Guinevere and Lancelot, and started to follow the sound, but it moved here and there like the wind around the forest. It was really the witch, Morgana le Fay. The laughter led them back to Camelot, and they saw Guinevere and Lancelot up on the battlements.

Mordred ran up the tower but the door at the top was locked. He broke the door open and fourteen knights clambered two by two into the room. Lancelot fought them all bravely, Agravain died, and Gawain's brothers too, ten knights died in total in the fight. Lancelot escaped, but Guinevere was left behind. Her punishment would be death, by burning.

Crossword

Across

1. What Noah sailed in.
3. Merlin has ________ powers.
7. Lightbulbs are screw fixing or ______?
8. It shows you where to go.
9. A plate, one of the 13 treasures.
11. Arthur's wizard.
14. Not ever.
15. A plant stalk.
17. A follower of a pop group.
18. A jousting spear
20. A knight rides one.
21. Arthur's lance.

Down

2. Arthur's friend from childhood.
3. Religious monastery man.
4. Get together.
5. Arthur's castle.
6. Once round a track.
7. One of Arthur's battles.
10. After sixth...
12. The Lady of the Lake.
13. Legendary King.
16. This is one.
17. Morgana le_____.
19. Neither this _____ that.

the Lost Land of Lyonesse

Sir Tristan came from Lyonesse, the mysterious land believed to be under the sea between Cornwall and the Isles of Scilly. The Saxon Chronicle says it was sunk on Nov 11th 1099, after a very high tide. Lyonesse had 140 churches, and it's said you can still hear the church bells ringing on a stormy night. Some say Merlin flooded the land to help Arthur escape Mordred.

Legend has it that the sole survivor of the flood was a man called Trevelyan and his white horse. The Trevelyan family have a horse emerging from the waves on their coat of arms.

St Michael's Mount, the island in Mount's Bay, has a Cornish name which means 'Hoary Rock in the Wood'. Remains of a sunken forest have been seen in the water. Perhaps there was land where now there is sea?

The Isles of Scilly are believed to be the mountains of Lyonesse. At some low tides three of the islands are joined, with causeways between them. Also walls can be seen going out into the sea. A reef called Seven Stones, between the Isles and the mainland, is believed to be the capital of Lyonesse, the City of Lions. In Cornish folklore the Seven Stones were called "The Town" by fishermen, who have hauled up windows, doors and household things in their nets.

How many churches can you count?

Lancelot and Guinevere

The following morning a great bonfire was built. Mordred chained poor Guinevere to a stake. At first the damp fire would not light. Mordred snatched a tinder and thrust it deep into the woodpile. As the flames started to rise, Guinevere cried "Lancelot, help me!" Before anyone could move, Lancelot galloped over, cut the stake with his sword so the chains fell free and swept Guinevere onto his horse. When Arthur was told of her escape, he secretly wept tears of joy.

Arthur, Mordred and Gawain went to hunt Lancelot down. Gawain wanted revenge for his brothers' deaths. They surrounded his castle for months but the walls were too high to get in. One day Lancelot called down to Arthur and Gawain. "No-one has ever taken this castle, and no one will. I have no quarrel with you and will not kill my king and my friend". But Gawain and Mordred refused to make peace, so Lancelot, resigned to battle, blunted his own lance and dulled his own sword. He told his knights to spare Arthur and Gawain, and then they rode from the castle to battle. Arthur held his lance and charged at Lancelot, who hit it with his shield, knocking Arthur to the ground. But instead of killing Arthur, Lancelot took his hand and pulled him to his feet. "Forgive me. Take Guinevere back, she still loves you". Arthur remembered all the brave deeds Lancelot had done for him and could not draw Excalibur against him. Gawain appeared and charged at Lancelot, but Lancelot dropped him to the ground with a mighty blow.

Merlin's Prison

Merlin fell in love with Nimue, the Lady of the Lake. He recklessly taught her magical secrets, which she used to imprison him.

Deep in the woods of Paimpont, Brittany, France, in the legendary Forest of Brocéliande, stand two ancient battered stones. This is all that remains of Le Tombeau de Merlin or "Merlin's Tomb" which the Bretons claim to be Merlin's everlasting prison. Now the monument is mostly destroyed. People say the landowner was looking for the treasure said to be hidden there.

the thirteen treasures

Merlin the Magician is also believed to be in a magical glass castle on Bardsey Island, North Wales. He is surrounded by the Thirteen Treasures of Britain. A gnarled and twisted apple tree is the only survivor of an orchard that the monks planted 1,000 years ago. The ancient tree is close to a cave where King Arthur and Merlin are believed be buried. 'Afal' is Welsh for apple, and some believe that is how Avalon got its name.

Can you find the magical 13 treasures in Merlin's cave?

1. **The Sword** If a nobleman used it, it burst into flames from its hilt to its tip.
2. **The Hamper** If food for one was put in, food for a hundred would be found.
3. **The Horn** Supplied whatever drink might be wished for.
4. **The Chariot** Would take you quickly anywhere.
5. **The Halter** Any horse you wish for you find in the halter.
6. **The Knife** Could be used by twenty-four men to eat.
7. **The Giant's Cauldron** A coward's meat would never cook but meat for a brave man would cook quickly.
8. **The Whetstone** Sharpen a brave man's sword with it, it would kill any man. A coward's would be blunt.
9. **The Coat** If a nobleman put it on, it would fit; if a peasant, it would not.

10-11. **The Crock and the Dish** Any food wished for would be found in them.

12. **The Chessboard** The silver pieces play by themselves.

13 **The Cloak of Arthur** Whoever was under it could not be seen.

Mordred and the Messanger

Arthur told Mordred to take his army home, but Gawain never forgot his oath to kill Lancelot and brooded as he recovered from his injury. One morning as Lancelot was looking down from the castle, Gawain rode up in full armour. "Defend yourself or die dishonoured!" Gawain cried.

When Lancelot reluctantly rode out to meet him, a messenger was talking to Gawain. Arthur was by his side. The message said "By the grace of god, I Mordred, natural son of Arthur, son of Uther Pendragon, heir to the kingdom of Logres, hereby declare that King Arthur is dead. Long live the king". The messenger had crept out of the castle unseen with the note, and warned Arthur and Gawain that evil Mordred was raising a large army.

Arthur thought back to the night in the woods on the day he had found Excalibur. He had been enchanted and thought he was with Guinevere when in fact it was one of the witches. Mordred must be their child. He ordered all his knights and soldiers to form an army and march on Camelot. Lancelot sadly said that he could not join him. He had decided to become a monk and would never wield his sword again.

Hidden knights

Can you find the knights in the box hidden in the sentences below?

My go-cart hurtles along the track
The SS Tremor dredged the ocean bed
In bed I've read a book
Show respect or else
Canoe or kayak?
The jousting era interests me
Cleric adores cake
To rob or steal is bad
Our chapel lease is long
The psychiatrist angered him

Bors
Geraint
Arthur
Mordred
Cador
Pelleas
Tristan
Bedivere
Ector
Kay

the draco

Colour me in

The draco was a flag that Arthur took into battle. It had a metal head of a dragon, and a material tube body that would flutter and flap as if the dragon was alive. When the horseman rode into battle at full speed the wind rushed into the dragon's mouth, filling out the tail and making a terrifying shrieking sound!

King Arthur in battle, with a draco, from a 14th century drawing.

Geoffrey of Monmouth mentions the dragon standard of Arthur's army. It was flown to mark a safe place at the battle for tired and wounded warriors to go to find water and have their wounds bandaged.

Was Arthur a Sarmatian?

Sarmatian and Alanian prisoners were sent to Britain in 175CE by the Romans. Marcus Aurelius sent them to help him fight. They lived in camps outside the Roman forts at Chester and elsewhere. They fought on horseback which was unusual in Britain then. It is thought Arthur could have learnt his horseman skills from them. They were dressed in scale armour. These tombstone fragments were found at Chester in 1890. They show a Sarmatian horseman holding a draco!

A Parley

Arthur and his army marched towards Camelot and a messenger arrived from Sir Bedivere to tell them that Mordred's army was a short distance away, at Camlann.

"Why does that name worry me?" thought Arthur. He lay awake and as dawn arrived a shape appeared in the mist—The Lady of the Lake. She told Arthur "Do not fight Mordred, thousands of knights will die if you do. Make a truce, save yourself and meet him another day". Then she disappeared as if in a dream.

King Arthur sent Sir Bedivere to organise a talk with Mordred. A parley agreed, both men took soldiers down to the meeting. "No one throw a spear unless you see one of their swords raised", warned Arthur.

Arthur offered to share his kingdom with Mordred, warning that if they fought today and he was killed, Mordred would be hunted down. Arthur turned his horse to canter off but Mordred shouted "No!" The noise made his horse rear and a snake crawled out beneath him. In a second Mordred had drawn his sword and sliced the snake in two. In panic, Arthur turned and looked towards his men. The earth trembled with the sound of their horses charging towards them, into battle. It was too late for peace.

Wordsearch

Can you find Arthur's brave knights in this wordsearch?

Lancelot
Bedivere
Gawain
Kay
Galahad
Percival
Mordred
Bors
Ector
Tristan

C	M	E	L	I	T	B	O	R	S
F	L	G	A	L	A	H	A	D	H
X	B	E	N	U	T	O	R	L	M
P	E	R	C	I	V	A	L	Y	O
U	D	W	E	G	I	O	A	L	R
G	I	Y	L	R	A	K	N	P	D
M	V	E	O	S	T	W	S	L	R
A	E	C	T	O	R	Y	A	D	E
T	R	I	D	C	P	O	N	I	D
P	E	L	T	R	I	S	T	A	N

King Arthur - did he exist?

St Gildas wrote the only surviving British book written in the time Arthur lived. It doesn't mention Arthur. But a later book "The Life of St Gildas" by Caradoc of Lancafam says that Arthur knew Gildas, but they had argued. Is that why he wasn't in the book? Or was it because he just didn't exist?

Gildas didn't mention many people in his book, except Ambrosius, who he liked. If he left out other important people, he could easily have ignored Arthur too. He mentions the Battle of Badon, but doesn't say who led the armies.

Arthur's legend was certainly strong even before Geoffrey of Monmouth's book in 1136. A book written in 1146 by Hermann of Tournai tells a story about nine religious men from France who went on a trip to England in 1113. Visiting Bodmin in Cornwall they were told they were in the "Lands of King Arthur" and shown two local sites, Arthur's Chair and Arthur's Oven. A man with a withered arm came to them wanting to be healed, and in conversation said that King Arthur still lived. The visitors laughed at him, a big fight broke out, and it needed an armed force to break it up! No one knows where the 'chair' and 'oven' were from the story. They are probably on Bodmin Moor. See if you can find them!

Colour the knight in using this colour chart

1 = light grey
2 = dark grey
3 = black
4 = brown
5 = red
6 = pink

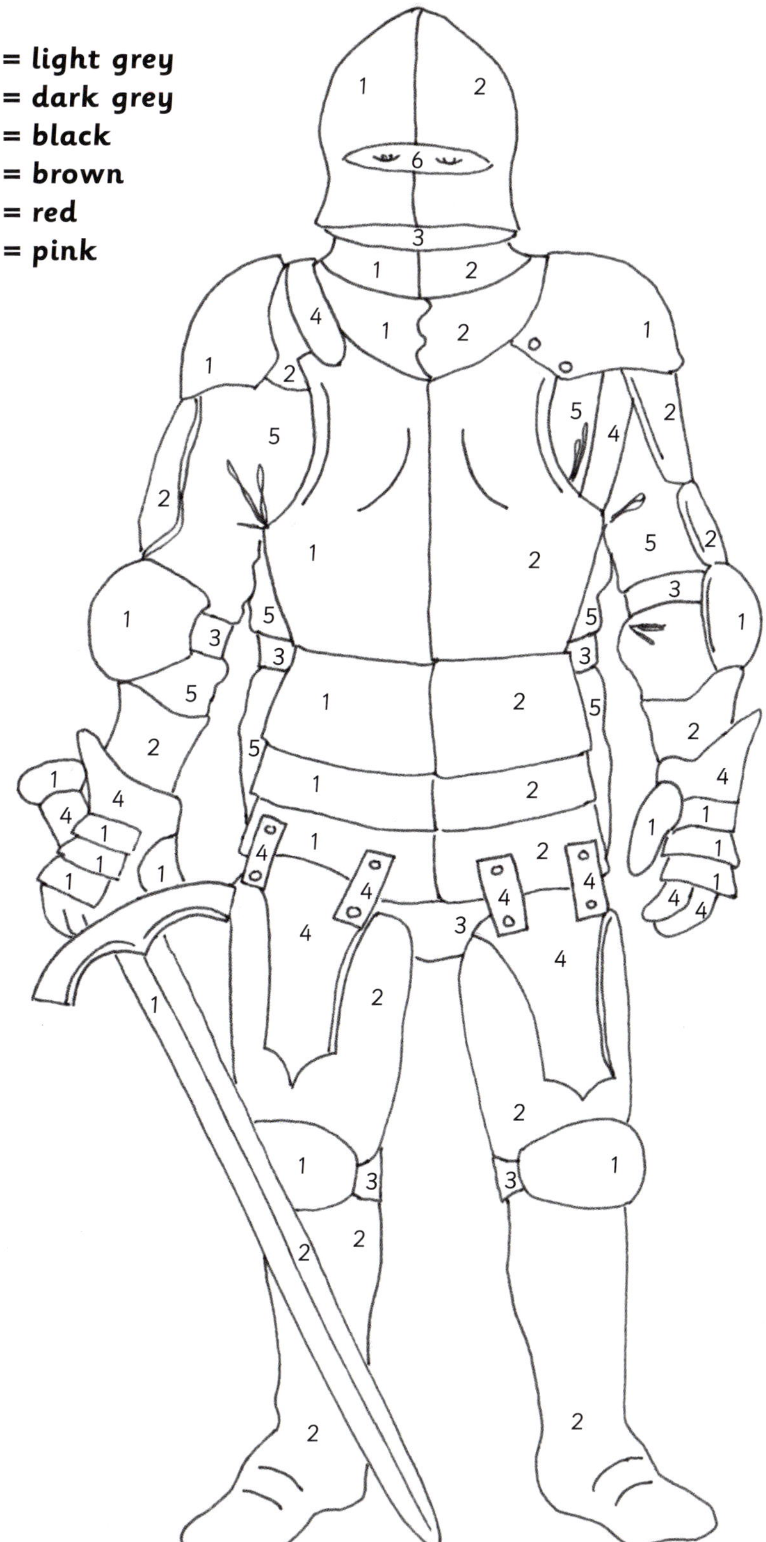

The Battle of Camlann

The river at Camlann ran red with blood. At dusk only a few knights remained standing. Sir Bedivere was wounded but alive. Mordred came staggering towards Arthur. "Fight!" called Arthur. But Mordred did not want to fight now. His men were dead. Morgana had left him, there was no one left to crown him. Excalibur hummed angrily and Arthur swung at Mordred's head but caught the sword in the ground. Seeing his chance Mordred ran at Arthur and magically Excalibur lifted free and ran through Mordred. He fell onto Arthur and died. Sir Bedivere found the wounded Arthur. "I am dying, carry me to the woods, there is something I must do before I die", Arthur gasped. Bedivere tried to carry him, but he was too weak and he laid him down by a tree. Arthur said "Then you must go in my place", and gave Bedivere the sword to throw into the Lake.

Through the trees Bedivere saw the moonlight shining on the water. He went to the lake, but then worried that if Arthur recovered, he would need the sword. So he hid it by the lake and returned to his King. Arthur asked "Did you throw it?" Bedivere lied "It fell with a splash and was gone". Arthur replied angrily "Then I do not believe you, Bedivere. Go back to the lake and throw it in".

King Arthur Quiz

1. Who was Arthur's father?
   a) Merlin
   b) King Harold
   c) Uther Pendragon

2. What is Arthur's famous sword called?
   a) Excalibur
   b) Ron
   c) Dave

3. Which knight sat in the seat marked 'Perilous'?
   a) Sir Galahad
   b) Sir Ector
   c) Sir Mordred

4. Who was King Arthur's wife?
   a) Elaine
   b) Guinevere
   c) Helen

5. Who is Arthur's magician friend?
   a) Sir Lancelot
   b) Morgana le Fey
   c) Merlin

6. What was Arthur's castle called?
   a) Camelot
   b) Camlann
   c) Astolat

avalon

Glastonbury in Somerset is believed by many to be the legendary isle of Avalon. Famous for its beautiful apples, it is where King Arthur's sword Excalibur was forged and where Arthur was taken after the Battle of Camlann.

Glastonbury was certainly an important holy centre. Joseph of Arimathea, Jesus's great uncle, is said to have come to Glastonbury and brought the holy grail with him. In the 12th century a grave was found with two bodies, believed to be Arthur and Guinevere. An inscription on a cross found in the grave said "His lacet Arthurus, rex quondum, rexque futurus" Here lies Arthur, the once and future king". The inscription is said by different people to have said different things. Nowadays, most people think the graves were a fake by the monks who wanted money to rebuild the abbey after a fire. But back then King Edward 1 and Queen Eleanor, who were keen on the Arthur stories, went to the reburial. This gave it great importance.

Guinevere's Prison?

In Caradoc's 'Life of St. Gildas', Gildas travels to Glastonbury Abbey when Melwas was king of the summer region. Glastonbury was being attacked by Arthur, because Melwas had captured Guinevere.

Archeaologists found at the top of the Tor a settlement from Arthur's time, that appears to be the stronghold of a local chieftain, perhaps a hilltop prison? Could wicked Melwas have hidden Guinevere here? The graves of two 6th century teenagers were also found on the Tor.

Apples of Avalon

Can you find the 8 hidden apples?

The Once and Future King

Bedivere went back to the lake, but once again could not bring himself to throw the sword in. Such a noble sword, and if Arthur died, it would remind Bedivere of him. So he hid it once again.
"What did you see Bedivere?"
"The ducks scattered and water rippled across the lake".
"Liar. Must I do it myself?"
Bedivere was sorry and this third time he threw the sword into the lake. A woman's hand broke the water, caught the hilt of Excalibur and pulled it down under the water. Bedivere watched, astounded.
"A hand reached out and caught the sword, Arthur".
"Well done", Arthur let out a long sigh.

The trees parted and three women came towards them, lifted Arthur as though he weighed nothing and put him in the barge they came in. "We are taking him to Avalon. His wound will be healed and he will sleep until he is needed again". The mysterious barge floated away into the darkness.

King Arthur lies there until this day, like Merlin, sleeping and waiting to save his land in its hour of greatest need. Arthur, once and future King.

Answers

Page 3

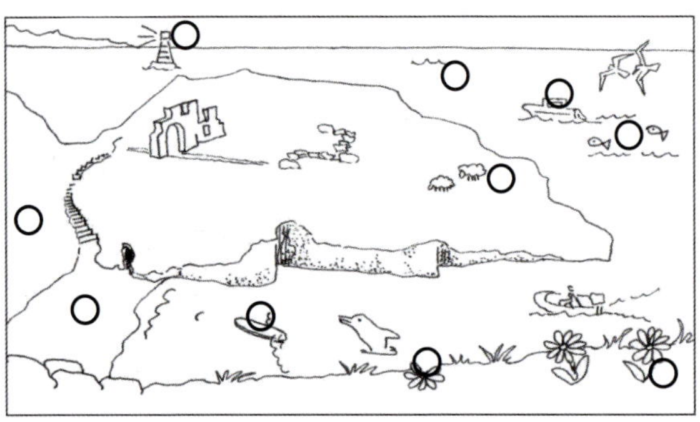

Page 4

Page 5, b

Page 6

miner	merl	limn	rem
liner	mien	nil	nim
limen	mire	men	ern
limner	rile	ire	rei
miler	lier	mel	rin
mile	lien	lie	lei
mine	lire	rim	lin
line	riel	mir	me
rein	emir	mil	mi
lime	rime	elm	em

Page 8

Loyalty	Faithfulness
Prowess	Skill in battle
Largesse	Generosity
Justice	Being fair and reasonable
Nobility	Noble birth or fine qualities
Courage	Bravery
Defence	Protecting from attack
Humility	Modesty

Page 9 Mordred, Arthur, Lancelot